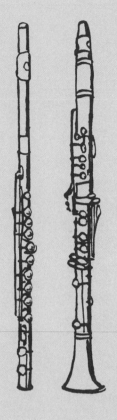

Seventy-Eight Duets

for FLUTE and CLARINET

by HIMIE VOXMAN

PUBLISHED IN TWO VOLUMES

VOLUME I (Nos. 1 to 55)

Easy-Medium

VOLUME II (Nos. 56 to 78)

Advanced

RUBANK®

HAL•LEONARD®
CORPORATION
7777 W. BLUEMOUND RD. P.O. BOX 13819 MILWAUKEE, WI 53213

Preface

Duet playing affords the student the most intimate form of ensemble experience. The problems of technique, tone quality, intonation, and ensemble balance are brought into the sharpest relief. Careful attention must be given to style as indicated by the printed page and as demanded by the intangibles of good taste.

The duets from the eighteenth century present many problems in the interpretation of ornaments. In the first volume the eighteenth century duets include those by various anonymous composers, and the Bachs, Boismortier, Dietter, Handel, the Mozarts, and others. In the advanced volume, in addition to the works of Bach and Mozart, those by Geminiani, Muffat, Quantz, Rameau, and C. Stamitz are in this category. In general, trills written before the year 1800, and probably many written thereafter, should begin with the note *above* the principal note. The symbol ∿ is *not* a mordent in eighteenth century music, but a short trill.

For a more detailed treatment of the embellishments the performer is referred to the article on "Ornamentation" in the fifth edition of Grove's *Dictionary of Music and Musicians*, or the *Harvard Dictionary of Music*.

The author wishes to express his gratitude to the libraries of the *British Museum* (London), and the *Bibliothèque Nationale* (Paris), for the use of collections of wind music found in these institutions.

Himie Voxman

Giguetta

BACH

Barcarolle in Canon

HALVEN

Bourrée

MUFFAT

Air
from Second French Suite

BACH

Gigue
from Second French Suite

BACH

Bourrée II
from First English Suite

BACH

Rigaudon

RAMEAU

La Joyeuse

RAMEAU

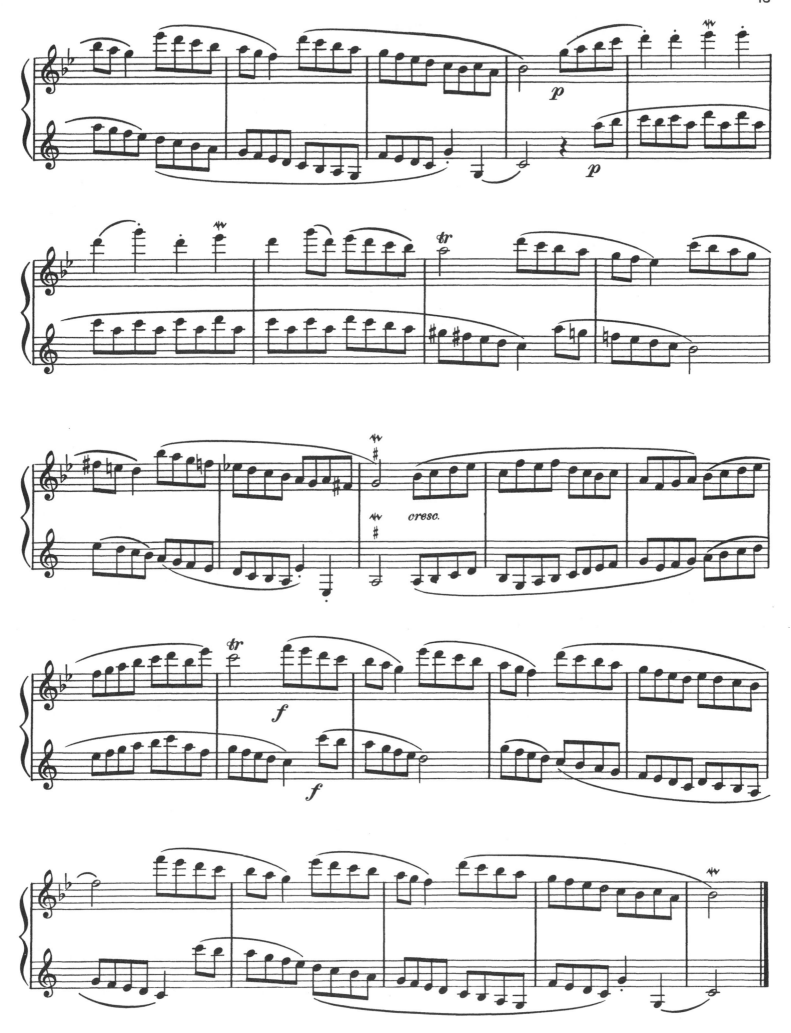

Arietta

PAUL KOEPKE

Duo No. 7

GEMINIANI

Six Little Preludes
No. 6

BACH

Rondino

PAUL KOEPKE

RICHTER

Duo No. 2
(K. 424)

MOZART
(adapted)

VARIATION II

VARIATION III

VARIATION IV
Allegretto

Little Prelude No. 12

BACH

Divertissement No. 2

RICHARD HERVIG

Allegretto (quasi waltz)

Duo No. 6, Op. 19

C. STAMITZ

Duo No. 1, Op. 46

G. KUMMER

Little Prelude No. 5

BACH

Duo No. 4

QUANTZ

Night Piece

ELDON OBRECHT

Duo No. 1

BEETHOVEN

attacca RONDO

RONDO
Allegretto [Vivace]

Rondo da Capo al Fine

Andante and Menuetto

MOZART
(18th Century Arrangement)

VARIATION III

Tempo di Menuetto